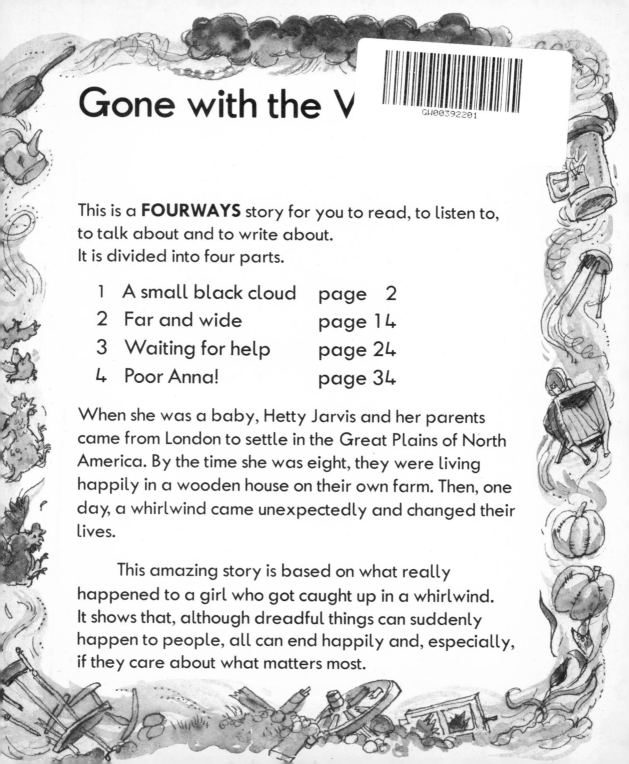

Gone with the V

This is a **FOURWAYS** story for you to read, to listen to, to talk about and to write about.
It is divided into four parts.

When she was a baby, Hetty Jarvis and her parents came from London to settle in the Great Plains of North America. By the time she was eight, they were living happily in a wooden house on their own farm. Then, one day, a whirlwind came unexpectedly and changed their lives.

This amazing story is based on what really happened to a girl who got caught up in a whirlwind. It shows that, although dreadful things can suddenly happen to people, all can end happily and, especially, if they care about what matters most.

1 A small black cloud

The morning had been misty but, after lunch, it became
so hot and sultry that Hetty and her mother went outside
and sat in the shade of the farmhouse. Mrs Jarvis rocked
to and fro and darned her husband's socks. Hetty, aged eight,
sat on a stool dressing her doll, Anna. The pink frock was
so tight that it wasn't easy pushing Anna's arms into the sleeves.
So Hetty was cross.

"I wish Anna wouldn't keep saying, 'Mamma! Mamma!' each time
she leans over," she said. "I like her to say 'Mamma!' when she's
looking at me. But it sounds silly when she has her back to me."
She tugged at the sleeve and pushed her doll sideways.

'Mamma! Mamma!' said Anna.

Then Mr Jarvis had made a house of sods, and that's where
they had lived during the first spring and summer while he planted
and harvested the first crop of corn. When he had sold the corn,
he used most of the money to buy a wagon-load of timber planks
with which to build a better house.

It had been a hard struggle to make a living.
But they'd made the wooden house into a comfortable home
with the few things they'd bought in America and the things
they'd brought with them from England.

"It's so dull here," Hetty complained to her mother. "There's nobody to play with. Nobody ever calls. Well, hardly ever, except for the mail-man. I wish a dustman would call now and then. And wouldn't it be nice if the dustman was Grandpa?"

'Mamma! Mamma!' quacked Anna, and they both laughed.

But Hetty went on complaining, "When I have a little girl I'll have nothing to tell her. You were lucky living in London."

The afternoon had become even hotter. It was so still. No breeze stirred the corn. Even the wind-pump had stopped squeaking. "I think everything's gone to sleep, Mother," said Hetty.

But Mrs Jarvis didn't answer. She'd gone to sleep too.

Corn grew on three sides of the farmhouse. It had already grown taller than a man, and yet its long leaves and cobs were still green.

While her mother slept, Hetty went on talking softly to herself. "We're sitting in a sort of box," she murmured. "Three walls of the box are green and the fourth is white."

She looked up at the cloudless sky and said, "Our box has a big blue lid. That's why we can't see or hear anything very much. That's why it's so dull here. Oh, how I wish the holidays were over and I was back at school even if I have to walk two miles to get there! At least there are ten other boys and girls to play with. I wish Father would buy me a pony so that I could ride to school over the fields."

Hetty sighed. She knew that her father could not afford a pony. They still didn't have a carpet or a second oil-lamp for upstairs, and her mother hadn't had a new dress for years.

Hetty stood up and sat Anna on the stool. Then she went off round the farmhouse. It was just as she had said. The box had three green walls of corn and the white wall of the house.

But the front of the house was different. Mrs Jarvis had dug and planted a little garden where she grew a patch of pumpkins and water-melons. Beyond that stood an empty wagon. Agrippa, the dog, lay asleep beneath it in a patch of shade; he was still tied to a wheel. Nearby a line of washing hung from two posts. Further away was the lavatory, a little wooden hut built over a pit. Then there was the big red barn and a few hens scratching about in its shade.

Hetty stood by the front door and looked across past the wind-pump to see if her father was in the fields. Yes, there he was, far away by the river. She waved, but he didn't look towards the house. He was shading his eyes and looking at something she could not see because of the tall corn.

As Hetty turned towards the door, she stumbled against
the big box her mother had dragged outside so that she could
scrub its inside. It was the box in which they had put things
to be safe on the long trip from London to the Great Plains of
North America. Things like the kitchen clock, a framed photograph
of Grandma and Grandpa, a picture of Queen Victoria, a cookery-book,
a patchwork quilt, and Mother's white wedding dress.

As she looked, a shadow crossed the box and Hetty turned
to see why. But everything was as still as a picture on a wall.
Even the hens had stopped scratching and had joined Agrippa
under the wagon.

Then she saw that the shadow had come from a small black cloud
crossing the sun.

Suddenly, squawking and clucking, the hens rushed back into the hot sun. They scurried madly all over the place, and Agrippa began to drag at his rope and to yelp.

Hetty ran beyond the little patch of pumpkins and water-melons to see what was happening. She ran beyond the red barn and stood by the wind-pump. From there she could see her father unharnessing his horse from the hay wagon. Then he sprang on Trigger's back and began to ride very fast towards the house.

What could it all mean? The small black cloud! The scurrying hens and the yelping dog! Father galloping bareback!

Suddenly Hetty was very frightened. "Mother! Mother!" she shouted, and ran back round the house.

2   Far and wide

Mrs Jarvis was awake and darning socks again when Hetty dashed back to tell her what she'd seen.

"Goodness me!" she exclaimed. "Why get so excited? Have you never seen a black cloud before? Let's hope it's going to drop rain on our fields and isn't just passing over. We badly need some rain to swell the corn cobs. As for the hens, who can tell what goes on in a silly hen's head? Let one run off squawking and they all run off squawking. And if Agrippa is yelping it's because the hens woke him in the middle of a nice dog-dream."

"But what about Father?" Hetty insisted. "Why is he coming? It's not supper-time, and he always brings the wagon home."

"Oh, he's probably forgotten some tool or other," her mother calmly replied. "Or maybe he can't wait until supper-time to see us. He was in a hurry to get married. He was in a hurry to get to America. I expect he's hurrying to tell us that next week we're all going back to London. His second name should be Hurry not Harry."

They laughed and Mrs Jarvis put down her sock. "Ah well!" she sighed. "Let's go and take the washing in before your black cloud rains on it."

Hetty followed her mother round the house until she came to the big box by the front door. Again she looked timidly about her. The patch of pumpkins and water-melons was just as it had been, Agrippa was asleep again and the hens had joined him under the wagon. The sails of the wind-pump were still, and so was everything else.

But the dark cloud had come from behind the wall of corn and was now plain to see. It had grown bigger and blacker and, as Hetty stared, it began to spin. Then a big bending funnel swayed down from it, turning and twisting until it reached the ground like a thick rope coiling and uncoiling.

Hetty looked on in amazement as the spinning, twisting tunnel
reached down to a haystack and sucked it in like a mouthful
of food. One moment the stack was there and the next it was gone.

Then Mrs Jarvis turned, took one swift look and shouted to the
staring girl, "Hetty! Hetty! It's a twister, a whirlwind!
Your father must have seen it across the river. He was riding
to tell us. Quick! Get back to the house!"

"Open the door wider! Wider still!" Mrs Jarvis cried as she dragged the big box inside the house. "Quick, girl! In with you!"
And she pushed Hetty into the box. "Stay there and you'll be safe."

Then, as the whirlwind swayed towards the house, she threw herself against the door trying to shut it. Hetty had never seen her like this before. Her mother was always so calm. Now, as she threw herself against the door, she screamed, "Sid! Sid!"

And Hetty screamed, "Father! Father!"

But it was too late. Everything in the whirlwind's path
was sucked into its spinning funnel. It sucked up the lavatory,
the clothes on the washing-line, Agrippa the dog, the wagon,
the rocking-chair, the stool and Anna. And the hens.
There was a puff of feathers as a running hen was plucked bare.
Then, one after the other, they shot up like bullets.

As it plucked everything into the air, the whirlwind wailed,
'Ah — h — h — h — h — h — h — h — h — h — h.
Then all became black as night. But it was a more awful blackness.

Inside the box Hetty heard this wailing. Then the sound changed to the beat of a big drum. Boom! Boom!
Then it changed again and hundreds of fists began hammering at every wall so that the windows rattled as though they were alive. The floor trembled, the box shook. It seemed as if the house was about to be torn up by the roots.

Blackness and noise! The little girl put her hands over her ears to shut out the din. Then the floor heaved like a wave beneath her and the box lid fell.

It became quite still. Something yet more horrifying was about to happen.

Like a big hand reaching down from the sky, the whirlwind scooped up the farmhouse. As easily as a gardener lifts a plant from the soil, it sucked the house into the air.

At first the house rose without a shake or a shudder. The kitchen clock went on ticking and not even a single teacup rattled. It was astonishing!

Then, when the house was as high as the top of a tree, it began to spin. Everything inside began to spin too, the beds, the cupboards, the table, the cups and saucers, the clock, the picture of Queen Victoria, Hetty crouching in the shut box and Mrs Jarvis lying against the locked door.

Then the house burst — first in, then out.

Glass burst from its windows, windows burst from its walls, walls burst into hundreds of planks, thousands of nails. The long stove-pipe flew up like a spear, the stove dropped like a bomb. Beds, chairs, pictures, pots, pans, knives, forks, brushes, boxes shot out and fell to the fields below.

The stair-case to the upstairs rooms came last of all. It went round and round like a big arm waving. Then it struck the ground. Crash!

And the hens? For the first time in their lives they became birds. They flapped like mad as their fat bodies dragged them down to bump into the dust. And what a row! It seemed as if they were all boasting about their wonderful wings. Yes, even the plucked hens!

Last of all came the curtains, the sheets and the clothes (still hanging on the line). They fluttered like flags across the sky in the track of the storm. Then they dropped gently upon the distant fields of the next farm and the farm after and the farm after that.

The farmhouse and everything it had contained was scattered
far and wide. As for the big box, when it landed with a thump,
it rolled over and over. When it stopped its lid was on top
so that its label was plain to see.

3   Waiting for help

Hetty lay in the box. She didn't cry. Everything had
happened too swiftly for that. She said to herself, 'Well,
here I am. I've been up and now I'm down. I haven't broken any
bones, and my ears are fine because I can hear a hen squawking.
My eyes are fine too as I can see a chink of daylight through
a crack in the lid. So now let's see what's happened.'

Hetty lifted the lid and looked around. She saw her mother lying quite still no more than three strides away. All her hair-pins had fallen out so that her long hair hid her face and came down to her waist. Her skirt and apron were above her knees and one leg was twisted beneath her.

Hetty managed to climb out of the big box but, each time she stood up, she fell down. Spinning round and round inside the whirlwind had made her dizzy.

She tried again to stand but, as soon as she left hold of the box, she fell. So she crawled on all fours across the soil to her mother's side.

There, she parted the hair from her mother's face and was astonished to see that it was as brown as an Indian's. The soil sucked up from the fields had been driven into the pores of her skin.

"Wake up, Mother!" she pleaded. But Mrs Jarvis didn't stir.

"Oh, Mamma! Mamma!" Hetty cried over and over again.

She stopped when she saw her mother's lips begin to move, and bent close to her face so that she could hear better.

"You sound like Anna," Mrs Jarvis said softly. "Thank goodness, you're safe. Oh dear, whatever has happened to me! My left leg hurts so much."

She didn't speak again for a while. Then she said, "Hetty, are you quite all right? Can you stand, dear?"

Hetty tried to stand. The dizziness had passed, and this time she did not fall. "Yes, Mother," she replied. "What shall I do?"

"You must go and tell your father where I am. He won't be able to see us amongst this corn."

As Hetty turned to go her mother called again softly, "Don't forget this place. Knock down the corn as you go. Make a path. And Hetty, dear, don't run off when you get to the edge of the corn. Just wait until someone sees you."

Hetty made a path through the corn by smashing down the plants as her mother had said. She had to go quite a long way before she reached the edge of the crop. When she got there she would have liked to have kept running until she found someone to help her mother. But she knew that she might not find the path again, and her mother might not be found until it was too late.

So Hetty did the hardest thing she had ever done. She waited.

Hetty had been waiting for a long time when she saw Agrippa, and Agrippa saw her. She called to the dog and he limped closer until she saw that he was dragging something at the end of his rope. When she had last seen him he had been fastened to the wheel of a wagon. Now the wagon had gone and the wheel had gone. Agrippa was tied to a single spoke.

Although Hetty called softly to him, he didn't approach any closer. His tail hung down and his ears lay back. Then he began to howl.

"Here, Grip," she called. "Good dog! Come here, Grip!"

But he backed away from her as if he was afraid of his name. Then he turned and limped out of sight, trailing the spoke behind him.

Hetty felt like crying but she knew that she must try to be brave for her mother's sake. Then she began to worry about her father. Where was he? Why didn't he come?

Hetty waited and waited. She watched the sun sinking
lower in the sky, and felt that she must go back to tell
her mother that nobody had come.

So she went back into the corn and carefully followed
the trail of smashed plants. It was like following a magic thread
into the middle of a fairy-tale forest.

At last she reached her mother and knelt by her side. Mrs
Jarvis didn't open her eyes. "Has nobody come?" she asked softly.

Hetty told her about Agrippa. To her astonishment her
mother smiled. "Poor Grip," she said. "He'll never have a ride
like that again. He must be the first dog that has ever flown.
He'll never let us fasten him to a wagon again."

But Hetty was thinking of something. What if the twister
had picked up her father too? What if he was lying in the fields
waiting for help?

"Oh Mamma!" she cried, "let me go and look for father.
I shall burst if I've just to stand still and wait."

"No, Hetty," said Mrs Jarvis. "You must keep calm and do
just as I asked you to do. You must wait by the edge of the corn.
Someone will come. People will keep looking for us. If they
don't find us today, they'll find us tomorrow."

"But what must I do if no-one finds us before it gets dark?" Hetty cried.

"Come straight back to me," her mother replied. "Call out and I'll call back. We'll stay together till morning. Go along now. Be a brave girl and do just what I've asked you to do. Grip's a good dog. He's afraid just as we are. But he'll come back. Dogs always come back. Next time he'll come right to you, you'll see. Don't go towards him. Stand still and he'll come to you."

So Hetty returned to the edge of the corn and waited.

Good girl!

4   Poor Anna!

And Mr Jarvis — what of him? Well, as he rode in frantic haste across the prairie to warn his family, he saw the house he had built rise into the air. Yes, rise into the air!

Then it began to spin. And, still gripping the spinning house, the rope of wind, swirling and howling down from the black cloud, turned. Mr Jarvis was now in the whirlwind's path.

He dragged at the reins and Trigger turned. But it was too late. Horse and rider were flung to the ground. Trigger, screaming with fright, scrambled up and raced off. But the farmer lay stunned.

And this awful visitor had not done with him yet. A moment later the house burst in, then out. In! Out! Part of the stair-case, whizzing round like a wheel, fell near him. It tottered first one way and then another before toppling gently across the little hollow where he lay.

When Mr Jarvis came to himself he was astonished to see the stairs above him. He struggled to free himself but was too weak from his fall to do much.

Just as he was feeling strong enough to try again, he felt a warm wet tongue licking his face. It was Agrippa. "Good dog," he said, and began to scrape away at the soil so that he could creep from beneath the timber.

'I must get out,' he thought. 'What has happened to my wife and Hetty? Were they in the flying house? Oh, if only I had a tool to dig with!'

Then he saw the spoke of the wagon's wheel still roped to
Agrippa's leg. It was just what he needed, and the dog stayed
still until Mr Jarvis untied the knot. Then he used the spoke
like a trowel to dig round the fallen stairs until he had made
a hole big enough to creep through. He was free again. But when
he looked for Agrippa, the dog was already limping off as fast
as he could.

The farmer had lived through an awful hour. He had seen
his house rise into the air and then be scattered far and wide
across the prairie. He had been stunned by a hard fall. And now,
as he looked across the fields, he was sure that his wife and
child must have been killed.

Mr Jarvis suddenly began to shout wildly, "Oh! Oh! Oh!"

After a time he became calm again. He saw that the red barn was still standing. Perhaps Hetty and her mother had crept into it and were huddled safe and sound amongst the hay!

Pale and dizzy, he stumbled off. But, before he reached the barn, he came upon a big hole in the ground. This puzzled him because there had been no hole there before. Then, in a corner, he saw his wife's clothes-mangle. Its frame was of iron. Evidently it had been too heavy for the whirlwind to carry off.

The hole was the basement of his house!

He turned away, went on and flung open the barn door. "Annie! Hetty!" he called, peering into the darkness. "Are you there?"

There was no answer. The barn was empty.

He stumbled back into the bright sunlight and leaned against a wall. Far off he heard Agrippa barking. The dog had not followed him but was standing near the place where Mr Jarvis had last seen him. And he barked and barked.

The farmer set off towards him, but as he approached, Agrippa ran a few yards further on, stopped and began barking again.

The frightened man still did not understand.

"Grip! Good dog!" he called. "Grip, here lad!"

But Agrippa wouldn't turn back.

"Come here, Grip. Good dog!" the farmer pleaded.

But it was no use. When the dog turned it was only to howl.

They were on the track that the whirlwind had taken. Here was a table leg, there the kitchen brush, a torn page from a book, a squashed pumpkin. Everywhere lay things that reminded Mr Jarvis of his lost home and family.

Suddenly he lost his temper and ran after Agrippa shouting, "You bad dog! Come here. Wait till I lay hands on you!"

Puffing and panting, Mr Jarvis ran on. Then he saw Hetty
standing at the edge of the corn. Agrippa was with her and was
leaping up and down. He had led the farmer to his waiting daughter.

Mr Jarvis hugged Hetty and patted Agrippa. Then, in Indian
file, he followed them both between the corn to his injured wife.

Mr Jarvis knelt beside his wife and took her hand.
He looked at her sadly but didn't speak. Then he began to weep.
      Hetty had never seen a man cry before and she began to cry too.
Soon all three of them were sobbing. Even Agrippa was howling.
  But that probably was because he was hungry.
"Where are we, Sid?" Mrs Jarvis asked.
"Not far from home," he replied. "Well, not far from where home was."
"Have we lost everything?"
"No, the barn's still standing. And the wind-pump."
"I mean all our things. Have they all gone with the whirlwind?"
"Almost everything," he said. "But you two are safe,
  and that's what matters most. I can build another wooden house.
  Until then, I'm sure some of the other farmers will help me
  to put up another sod house."

Hetty was astonished. After the terrible ride in the whirlwind she had supposed that her mother and father would leave the American Plains and return to London.

Her father guessed what she was thinking and said, "This is our home, Hetty. We've lost the house and almost everything in it. But the fields are ours. Back in England we should never have had a farm. We must stick it out.

"Now we must get your mother out of the corn. We must take her to the next farm and then send for the doctor. Go and find Trigger and harness him to the stone-boat. You'll find the stone-boat safe inside the big red barn. As for Trigger, he might still be a bit frightened from the whirlwind, but he's safe and sound too."

Hetty was pleased to be doing something useful, and so she ran off quite happily.

Trigger and the stone-boat were just where her father
had said. At first the frightened horse backed away from Hetty.
But she coaxed him slowly to the barn door and, ten minutes later,
he was harnessed to the stone-boat.

When Hetty returned with Trigger pulling the stone-boat,
Mr Jarvis had already made a splint for his wife's leg.
With Hetty's help, he carefully lifted Mrs Jarvis on to the
stone-boat and led it very slowly out of the corn.

By this time, nine or ten men, women and children
from nearby farms had come to see what had happened. Some were
just standing round the hole where the farmhouse had been.
Others were picking things up, and two men had even started to make a
pile of the scattered planks.

44

One little girl had found the twisted frying pan and
another had found the kettle. But everything made of pot, glass
or wood had been smashed.

Over there is a handle. But where is the cup?

There's a clock-face. But where is the clock?

There's a photo of Grandma and Grandpa. But where's the frame?

And here's a handful of feathers. But where's the hen?

When the two little girls saw Mr Jarvis leading Trigger,
they ran to the stone-boat. They stared at Hetty as if they
had never seen her before. The red soil had been driven into
the pores of her skin and she had a black eye. She limped, too,
because she felt like one big bruise.

"Oh, Hetty!" the girls cried. "You're safe. What happened
to you? Where were you when the twister hit your house?
Tell us all about it."

"I've been flying," she said. "Do you suppose I'm the first girl
ever to fly? And I flew in a box!"

Then Hetty stopped speaking because she saw Agrippa scratching in the soil. He had found a brass bead hanging from two bits of wire.

Hetty picked it up. Nothing else was left of her talking doll. Poor Anna! Gone with the whirlwind!

Then she swung the brass bead to and fro and, as it swung, she quacked softly, "Mamma! Mamma!"

Things to Talk and Write About

1   What made Mrs Jarvis talk about London when she was
    a girl.
    Write down some of the things she told Hetty.
    Think of ways of finding out what it used to be like where
    you live now, and make a book about your discoveries.

2   Describe the coming of the whirlwind and what
    happened when it scooped up the farmhouse. Use the
    same kind of language that the author uses to paint vivid
    word-pictures.

3   How did Agrippa help the family?
    What did Mr Jarvis say 'matters most'?
    Talk about what matters most in your life.

4   What do you think of Hetty?
    Would you have done things and felt as she did?

5   Find all the compound words in the story like whirlwind.
    Make a list of them and explain what they mean.

6   Write about this book in a way which would help other
    children to decide whether they would enjoy reading it.
    Using the same kind of descriptive language, write your
    own story with a happy ending about another kind of
    natural disaster such as a flood or an earthquake.